Four-Wheeler

&

Two-Legged

poems

Stephen Wing

with gratitude to
my Mother and Dad,
Peter, Robin, Dawn, Judith, Rich
and all my other teachers
for their patience and support

and thanks to
Katuah Journal, Street Heat,
Rural Southern Voice for Peace, CALC Report,
Scenezine, Black & White, *and* All Ways Free
for publishing some of these poems

ISBN   1-881891-00-3

Library of Congress
Catalog Card Number
92-82541

cover design
Robin Merritt
photography
David Christian Glueck
PRINTED ON RECYCLED PAPER

Four-Wheeler &
Two-Legged

for

my grandmother,

Anna Maude Muse

and

Asa, Lela, Jesse, Eli,

Massiel & Keffrén

her great-grandchildren

love,

Uncle Steve

I

SURFACE
MAGIC

For Walking

I thank you, God,
for giving me two big strong feet
    and four square limbs
    for walking

    Then let my possessions
    be scattered from me,
    let good friends multiply
    and disperse, let my big toes
    lead me on and on across the earth—

The wheeling sky knows
all my directions, it is going there before me,
    my companions the highways
    stride the horizons at my side

    I will follow this urge
    in my arm, love, to reach you
    though I reach with my
    cracked thumbnail, stagger
    on my blistered heel, though you
    come to your door and call me fool—

The concrete slab beneath bridges
is bed to me when some wild stormfront
    scatters my company of stars, save
    for the rare night's ride

    Scatter my ashes along any
    highway shoulder's cinder
    under floodlights or a full moon,
    let the traffic and the weather
    travel on without me when I'm gone—

May the angels
give me free winds for wings and the changing
    cloud-ranges to wander!

In the Oklahoma City Zoo
an Eagle Looked at Me

From the highest limb
of the tree in the cage his eyes caught
all the light of the Oklahoma sky
the way talons close on flesh:

Not caring to see if to see
          was only to see through,
not caring to fly if to fly
was to swoop for meat the keeper brought,
I spread wings for him
and flew against my own wire mesh.

Half-Veronica

The hitchhiker is mortal
          like the matador,
swinging his cape of cardboard
          and crayon
from the hip as lowered brows
          of chrome come
rumbling, the horns of the instant
          miss by inches
and tons of truck go by like eighteen
          thunders—

The hitchhiker is immortal
          like the bull:
he stands unswerving to meet
          every deadly pair of
sidestepping eyes

Surface Magic

Dear sleeping ones to westward,
at this moment one hour west
of dawn,
between the Agents of Light and
the Arsenal of Signs I look out
passing through
another town.
All the eastbound windows slumber on.

> *Roaming the rain-pelted woods*
> *deep inside me*
> *is a fear of black people*

> *Rooted*
> *in my black soil*
> *is a loneliness for women*

Sometimes I have to rest my mind
on the hard earth, remembering
darkness:
what the cave speaks. What the moon
illuminates. The light itself is
invisible all day,
waking only when
the running lights race my long asphalt shadow.

> *Something in me loves the dance*
> *of destruction,*
> *wrestling the power mower,*
> *wielding the woodmaul*

Darkness lives,
and never lives on only one side
of the border

Yes,
I remember the Not-Seeing of Zen,
the Way of the Crooked Shaman,
the Evangelists
of the Artificial Moon. I have not
forgotten the bulletproof limousines
of the Messiahs.
Take heart:
the earth's dumb gods are watching.

I can't do anything
right
therefore I am

Across
the electrified fence of my fear I offer you
the thing I lack

Sleeping ones, you only see these
headlights wash across your ceiling
hours before dawn.
My friends, you only know me by my
vanishing. If you were only with me!
What a privilege it is
to be riding west
this morning with the daybreak in my mirrors!

Inside I balance
at the tip of the highest
fir tree
in the Blue Ridge

Territory of the Wanderer

I.

I crept
through the spring woods

to the graveyard of the rusty cans

It seemed to be the place
I was looking for

In brown needles, among seedling pines

I left the mark of my passing,
territory of the wanderer

like this glittering water, passing through

2.

I move in the water
like an inflatable man, afraid
to let go my air

gasp for breath between gulps at the fountain

Yet I wade heavily through the air,
I am so much water

No wonder I can so rarely rest

Even here I detect a slight
decline and imperceptibly lean south

as clouds drift on sunlight and never feel the wind

3.

The water calls to me
in its own language, and I respond

The rain insists on anonymity

but fills the footprints and the worn places
with little mirrors of heaven

The snow falls unanimously sideways

and the sea swells and lunges with a steady
suicidal music, crashing up the shore

The river murmurs ceaselessly how famous I was

Rainbow on Wet Pavement

The rain god is smiling
on me again, and
I get wet

The clouds have come down
to sniff the highway
and leave their scent

and the oil of trucks
makes a rainbow on wet pavement
washing back into the ground

The old ones are with us

*The rivers travel through
our sleeping settlements
like always*

The Pilgrimage to Rest (and Travel On)

The canoe sang all the way
on the roof of the car
as if it remembered this highway

> North by the Pole Star
> a dark lake is draining south under the Dipper,
> slung like a hammock
> between the beaverdam and the waterfall
> but never resting

The canoe sang all night to the moon
as if remembering
the sound of water at the bows

> Leaping every minute from its granite lip
> into song, the water falls:
> stroke by stroke against the slow, perpetual
> adjusting of waterlevels
> from lake to lake, we paddle closer to its mist
> and thunder, step by step
> beneath our upturned keels we climb
> toward the northern divide

The moon calls down
to some memory of tide in us as we drive
under our upturned hull
against the wind of our chosen direction

> Rounding the rock face where the water falls
> we cease our paddle-talk
> to listen: up that steep ledge it calls us,
> to the level of the next lake
> where we'll stretch our tents on their poles
> and tie our hammocks
> to rest a day while the canoes sleep, upturned
> on a granite shoulder

Some night years from now a star will fall
reflected in that lost lake
and wherever we are we'll remember how
the song of falling water called us
one step higher in its long pilgrimage
downhill

Fire Over Illinois

The summer is defined by shade

The axe-head sings its arc,
its piece of the turning of day and night.
In ceasing it is useful.

The sun is falling slowly
into fire over Illinois

The rope is strong, but always
has to pay out some of itself
to get somewhere. Ending, it is useful.

The winter is a long shadow

That horizon burns inside
the wanderer at sunset

The book's pages turn, one by one,
the half-circle that gives life
to a name eroding someplace from stone.

The gaze turns like a leaf
toward the streetlight

There is no death, only shadow

To the Animal Tribes

Thank you, spirit of the deer tribe
for appearing in three cantering shapes
the color of woods-shadow, each
hesitating at the edge of the road
till they recognized us and bounded across,
vanishing into forest-light again
while we sat idling, incognito
in our tinted glass, disguised in our clothes
on our way to the council

Ever since we left blacktop
for the long sandy straightaway
into the forest, we kept passing the signs of war:
4x4's and double-wheeled
pickups parked along the ditches,
men with rifles and coolers in swivel chairs
on the roofs of their vans

And thank you, spirit of the snake tribe
for appearing in your intricate
armor, many-colored
pygmy rattler over a foot long
almost invisible in the brown grass
where a lake has disappeared
since the last time we met here to consider
the year to come

Men in Washington hold photographs
taken from satellites
up to the light, selecting "military
targets," experts on T.V.
recite their wagers, and
the factory where they make the bodybags
is hiring

Thank you, spirits of the infinitesimal frog
and phosphorescent green
grasshopper tribes, tribes of prickly pear,
palmetto and pine, spirit of the symbiosis
of live-oak and Spanish moss,
spirit of the osprey circling high above the branch
where we've tied our kitchen-tarp

Jetstreams overhead point the way
to the hotels of Disney World,
the sprinklers of Orlando,
the million engines of the empire
sucking the life out of the ground,
the miles of lights
burning their nightly quota of whatever time
is left

       And again, spirit
of the deer, for incarnating
out of the moonlight when we were
lost on the path, looking for this place—
so far ahead we couldn't tell who it was
gazing down the alley of darkness
till you recognized us a second time and turned
to vanish
       (Only then,
your sleek flank turning
in the full moon's ecstasy
deflected from the other side,
only then did we know you
friend and guide)

The Proprietor's Itch

The lights are on late
in the long chickenhouses tonight

The migrations of humans
must be a mystery to the birds

I am tracking the end of this yellow line

Like a man tunneling deep into himself,
I sit watching the road roaming on
under the headlights

o

Something walks the creaky ribs
of the house tonight

Leaves spiral down the awkward
staircase of a tree

The streetlight burns all night in the yard

Like a man balanced, trembling
on the peak of his roof
he gazes after taillights on the highway

o

The crack in his foundation accrues
its nightly interest

My flywheel spins out its
inevitable proof of itself

Even the coffin rots away at last

The trees live half underground,
roots branching out in the blackness, reaching
under the property lines

Bivouac Between Billboards

That's what happens when you
sit down suddenly
with the prospect of rest:
you grow rooted, content to sway
on some traveler's horizon
where the clouds are riding and soon
a season's leaves, even the birds
gone one day—

                    Little sister,
watching you speak solemnly
to your children, I grow homesick
for my own unborn ones and the nest
of summer grasses I may never weave

Here on this hump
scraped up by bulldozers, camped
in the eclipse of shadows
between two towering floodlit billboards,
I lean out with the high limbs
of the trees along my highway,
reconnoitering by the dance
of my candleflame

Small winds close to the earth
speak to me now that I
crouch among them,
they want me to carry messages
to the tops of mountains

The evergreens are turning brown
The cars go by crooning the song of
sleeping nations
The crickets sing their spells for dawn
Even the crow thinks he's singing!
Pouring the wax out of the candle,
I begin

Horizon in Motion

In the dead hour between radio stations
the passenger gazes out, and out, and suddenly
begins to see again:
                         rusting stallions
retired to a mountain pasture, wheelless ruins,
"Love" and "Peace" corroding
between the headlights of a psychedelic van

Days flick back like the yellow dashes
between lanes

           "Love," it said
in spray-paint on the overpass, a leap
of the heart, whoever hung over the bridge
catching the cold whiff of the can,
pumping that old desperation of the young,
"Love—"

           The passenger gazes ahead:
solid white and yellow lines hum every curve
in unison, that song that is a traveler's
only boundary

           The way is narrow
Even the body breathing at his elbow,
loose fingers cradling the wheel
cannot travel with him to this musing sunset, this
drowse of horizon

           "Peace," cautious
black capitals in the headlines again today,
hopeful and noncommittal, locked
behind the little window in the vending machine,
hostage to old men whose name for victory is
"Peace"

> But he remembers
the way a child's hand fell into his
as her daddy raced those mountain curves,
chasing the bastard that passed him, love as real
as the heat in the car against the cold pane—
an old man whose hand gripped his with a pulse
he couldn't tell from his own, true peace, silent
kindred after two hours' talk—

> *The gate is strait*
He closes his eyes and leans, breathing in, and begins
to feel again: cool wind is rushing by
on the other side of the glass

Whether that keyhole-slot in earth or
the spiral eye of the galaxy,
the passenger hurtles unerringly homeward
sometimes motionless, sometimes faster
than radar

Fugitive Come Home

Look up and
close your eyes. Do you
see the new stars
of the place this earth could be?

Look down now:
do you see
the strange feet of the fugitive
come home?

Now
look around.
Do you notice any unfamiliar
faces in your family?

Empire of View

Steps in the stone wall
lead me up under tangled bowers
into an arboretum of weeds, preserve
for every known species of bottle

Footprints, mark of any passing
animal, random shoes in single file:
humans walked here, upr ight, in tandem,
strung on that taut thread
civilization

A beaten carpet in the high grass
at the crest of my chosen city
throws a house of pure homesickness
to mountains and sky

Fire-circle, mark of the tr ibe
of humans in any wilderness:
bits of aluminum and glass catch sunset,
an untold decline come to light
in the narrow mud tr ack

I have taken a new city, just looking!
This vacant lot is home now,
this hilltop above the freeway is my wild bed
under the opening emptiness tonight

Around me shines my empire of distance and light

II

GHOST ANTELOPES ON THE HIGHWAY

The Homestead on Horn Mountain

Long ago
someone climbed to the top of this mountain
and dug a well.

This is the place, marked
by an elderly pine.
I part a way through the overgrowth
with my stick
to the black brackish water in its circle of stones.

This is mystery:
stone more ancient than the mountain, water
as eternal as all circles.
Someone lived here and drank that water
and disappeared under moss and bramble.
The ground is littered with rocks
of a fallen homestead.
The well is a shaft of memory sunk in the ground.

Turning to scribble a note to myself
I start to the sound
of a motor:
since I last climbed Horn Mountain somebody
has cut a road just above the old homestead,
I can see the cigarette
in the driver's hand as a yellow truck comes
rumbling past—

I duck below the bramble like the spirit of ruin
that haunts this place,
diving back down the black shaft
of undrinkable remembrance
past the names of mountains and roots of pines
down to the underground river of earth's long
forgetting.

O Beautiful
Fallen Mother of Acorns,
Goddess to Squirrels

For spacious skies

Standing to sing through the tears in my eyes,
a naked Indian among the lipstick
and neckties of the congregation,
I remember the stars fell like leaves above my mountain
the night I fasted, and firelight leapt
in the eyes of warriors when I sang to them.
The earth is beaten down
with dancing, in the blurred air
I hear drums—

God shed his grace

My blood is pulsing
through a stained light as we sing "Amen!"
and settle in our pews.
Gripping the smooth scrolled wood
so tightly in both hands that I have to shut my eyes,
suddenly I recognize the grain:
the tree I touched and grieved that night
I saw the lights of towns
burning up and down the valley
and found my song.

Under an Incandescent Sky

on the platform at Loyola
　　waiting for a late train, & the world
curves away under rectangular
　　　fluorescent panes,
　　riding the curve of the rails
　　　　　past the traffic light
　　　　　　changing
　　in the intersection below

The west is burning
　　　　Two towns evacuated
　　　The administration may soon abandon
its controversial "let burn" policy
　　　　Floods
in Iceland, mudslides in China,
　　　drought in the Sudan
　　　　　while the driest summer
in fifty years
blazes over the Midwest

And eight miles from Grand Canyon
　　National Park they still
　　long to sink their empty shaft
　　　into the Mother,
peddling their smug junkie's rationale
　　　　along with their poison:
　　　　uranium
　　　　　for a wilderness of lights,
　　the billion globes and tubes
　　　　　　of Chicago's dark
　　　　　　delusion
　　　　　flushed with
　　　　　　power

Sacrament of the Six-Pack

Sacrament of the six-pack
at quitting time:
toss ritually can by can
to the roadside
as you ride the four-lane
home—

>*Listen, it isn't enough*
>*to pick up the litter any more, that time*
>*has come and gone*

Like human teeth found
in the firepit
with charred animal bones,
blind couples
staring from old photographs,
your anonymous
empties—

>*Listen, no matter how deep*
>*they bury it for you, you paid for it,*
>*brother, it's yours*

Our memory in the earth's crust
will be this: junk of
every innovation, artifacts
abandoned to the past
that will outlast us, all those forms
in triplicate
                    (your last
will and testament is filed there,
and mine, and all we leave
behind—)

>*Listen, whatever wealth you*
>*pile up for your children, it will never be*
>*enough*

The Geologist's Box

Helping the geologist pack up his rocks
for the movers, the poet delves
through stratum on substratum of old news.

The legal notices mutter toothlessly to themselves.
The classifieds tremble full of secrets
desperate to be told. In the opinion pages, so many
lonely immortals lie petrified—

This rock is the crystal of a million years.
All the time we were pushing
erect, it was sculpting this shape from within.

The front-page headlines are the most pathetic:
tragedies wrung dry in the twist
of a pun, melodrama in clownface while inside
a shadowy crowd starves and grieves—

This rock holds the signature of some
ancestral skeleton. We have
evolved our own mute signs to survivors.

Each day before dawn the loaded trucks
distribute their stacks of print:
the news-stands, the coin-vendors, the slung
sacks of paperboys on bikes—

This rock was the knee of a dinosaur.
Like all things lifted and
abandoned, it's a piece of the earth now.

And under the landfills in vaults of decay
the advertisements feed bacteria,
rat-litters nest in the obituaries while tree-pulp
that was history turns back to tree-pulp—

This rock shows the strokes of the first
vertebrate to puzzle it out. How
make a tool without tools? How to start?

And the ink escapes its columns at last, grinning
photos weep across their captions,
percolating through ancient plastic to taint
the subterranean seeping of time—

The packed box is almost too heavy for one
geologist to lift. He marks it
FRAGILE in black ink, and we go back inside
for another beer.

Landscaper's Assistant Looks Down

All the modestly expensive,
lavishly landscaped
artificial gardens
of this overweight white man's back yard,
all the concrete and clipped grass,
beds of perennials around the long blue
pool-cover, holly trees
along the low brick wall, all of it
including my six bucks an hour,
all of it is worth
less than the four severed fingers
of a small, wet
brilliantly patterned toad
panting in the pinestraw, still in shock
from my too close,
too quick
shovel-thrust

The War Against the Trees

Of course you cut the tree limb back
to make way for the telephone wire,
of course you top and trim
the wild branches from the boy to make a soldier,
of course you fly miles
per second through the upper atmosphere to close a deal
that will cut short the century-long
breaths of the jungle, another million acres gone
to make paper and grow beef—

What kind of war is this
against the flowers of the valley of the Amazon,
against the tribes this wilderness
has civilized, against the songbirds who fly south
from your sealed window to winter here,
against the children who need
the exhalations of these green cities to live
when you are gone?

Of course it wasn't you who ignited a spark
in the tiny brain of the bulldozer,
who chanted the one formula
through its fuel line that could make it charge amok,
churning delicate foliage under tanktracks,
chewing down the towers of this ancient
capital of the trees—

The clues are everywhere.
Who ate the hamburger
out of that paper sack and left it there,
a greasy blossom of the parking lot?
Who crumpled that mediocre draft of a poem
only moments ago, tossed it like
a paper flower on the tomb of the spring
and split open the fresh ream?

Ghost Antelopes on the Highway

Repeat three times daily:
I have no effect on my environment.
My environment has no effect on me.
I have no effect on my environment.
My environment has no effect on me.
I have no effect on my environment.
My environment has no effect on me . . .

o

Ghost antelopes on the highway

Subdivisions for the dead

Coyote running the fence along the rim
of vision
though the driver never turns his head
quick enough to see

Evacuation Route
SEQUOYAH

(Cows in a little pasture
by the stream below the road, grazing
under the hum of the reactor—)

Shadows crawling out from under
the relics of daylight
This is their time
Low tide-pools in us already
starting to fill
with drought

while we go on
harvesting the whales

o

Ghost antelopes on the highway

Pesticides are rising in the wells
while we file through our turnstiles
at the end of the food chain

Turkey-buzzards circling high
on the supermarket pavement's heat
like a dark host

SCHOOL BUS

ENTERING

HIGHWAY

Choosing my sweet potatoes late
that night
from the supermarket bin,
I thought of my mother
Too late to try another call
but I was
forgetting the time zones again
Bugs were dancing
round the sack of onions I chose

In the birthing of a baby
you can see the turning of the world

The girls grow up
and marry their awkward lovers
and before you can forget, there she is
answering the baby's unbearable distress,
uncertain as you were
how much is love and how much is just
the turning

(Think back on all the rich
generations of timber
fallen and risen again on these hillsides
thick with nesting humans—)

The boys grow up
and marry the factory instead,
roll from their renegade dreams
at the rattle of the alarm, no matter
if the working man sleeps late into Saturday,
a secret piston pumps away in his chest
laboriously
turning the world

CRAFTY BEAVER
HOME CENTER

Framing
Drywall Special
Kitchens

Now Hiring

(The bulldozer's bright blade
splinters wood with crude
surgical precision as the turning tracks
crush whatever snaps back—)

We'll all
be elderly by and by,
stiff and forgetful, in debt
to the doctor and our disobedient bowels:
the clocks go faster as you slow down, they say
and your sphincter loosens
till the sure, uncertain hour of your absolute
relaxing—

All our animals and clowns
have deserted us
and gotten jobs in slaughterhouses
and saloons, selling us
the objects of our
unidentifiable desire

while our children's soft
skulls harden

○

Ghost antelopes on the highway

The landfills are piled high
on the cemeteries of the unborn

The owls hunt alleys in us glittering
deep in glass,
a forest of grey corpses
haunts the high country of the imagination

We Have Thanksgiving
Candy & Supplies

SAVE   DISCOUNT DRUGS

Slicing sweet potato for breakfast
next morning
I think of the slender knife they must have used
Dicing one half
sweet onion, I have to look out the window
remembering her strong talk
near tears
on the telephone

(The nuke's grey towers
stand invisible above the crowd
on the beach at Zion
like the monument to some defeated
late-movie monster

But at night they light it up
like a resort hotel
where ordinary folks can't go)

Like a hard pearl of nervous waiting
under her skin,
lonesome as a knot of ice and dust in space,
hungry as an unwanted child,
this thing grew in her:
an irritation deep in the tissue of her breast,
resin of her poisons,
pouch where she hid her
worry—

CAREFREE
Chemical
Re-Arranger

16 oz. $7.97

(Practically any one of us
would snap back at the fire
snarling down the stairwell
to save the babies deep in the burrow

What dark wind underground
pins us to our easychairs
in front of the late movie,
why do we let the babies sleep
so peacefully in that dark wind's shadow?)

Vietnamese voices on the train
Shining magic
marker on the vinyl seat
claiming territory
in some clandestine
war of adolescents

while we go on
burying our wounded

o

Ghost antelopes on the highway

Condominiums for the damned

The bison are returning in new,
invincible bodies
to thunder the fenced miles of Interstate

WE'RE SPENDING OUR CHILDREN'S INHERITANCE!

My foot on the pedal
as the gasoline flows
to its spark—

I have contributed my piss
to this toxic puddle, I have
flushed my yellow down its sick blue,
drunk on its smell of chemical

—we ride,
carousing these fresh scars
of our old, complicated
birth

I found a fiendish face
of flattened plastic among the litter,
I picked it up to carry home
to my cave of trophies and souvenirs

(Styrofoam, like bitter manna
strewn along the sidewalk, white against
the green lawn
                —a disposable ice-chest,
one bite gone, beginning its long
disintegration and ascent
to the ozone
                —a hole
the size of the U.S.A. above the pole now,
the supermarket headlines crow)

When they say they love their country,
only pay heed
how they care for the land

○

Still,
angelic genitals of mushrooms
split the blades of grass
nearby

LAST DAYS
BAPTIST CHURCH

Still,
flowers bloom like innocent
nipples on the afternoon

We shall rush like the sea
onto cold deserted beaches
again and again,
loving each other

while our elders drown
little by little
in air

Still,
on invisible wings the hummingbird goes
trusting the sunlight

In the burying of a body
you can see the turning of the earth

Visiting the Deer

Going up to visit the long view
at the top of the hill
today I have
travelled the deer-trails:
bending to duck under
where the deer duck under
branches,
leaping where the deer leap
dry ravines, coming at last
into open sky:
gazing down where the deer gaze
down on human hospitalities
with wild shy suspicion—

When I caught my breath
I looked down and saw only
the houses of my
neighbors, the loop of road.
Going back I travelled
as usual down the track of tires
in the dirt.

III

UMBILICUS

The Stones at Laurel Creek

The stones here are
shoulders and elbows of the lover I
looked for everywhere I travelled
to arrive here
                    poking through her
garment of rhododendron, shaped
by her rush of laughter, eddies
of attention

                    I feel her
enjoying my step best when I step
naked, enjoying it
                    Like the pause
when the fingers seem to listen to the skin
and forget which name the lover has
and what color the skin,
                    I bend
to soothe my hands on her tender grain

Through the slow, gigantic
pulse of sun in stone I suddenly
recognize her—

                    (but even that
is just a name
                    She lies
under every itch and movement of my foot
and I have only known her
by names)

Encounters out of the Body

You are a creature contained in your skin,
how can I feel you
still warm inside the shirt you gave me,
startling my cold skin?
What is it in the shape of the hills under
moon tonight, in this
reckless air that moves against my hand?
How can I hear your laugh
in every ring of the phone and every echo
of the last ring,
and feel the breath when the sound has died away?

Metronome

"This Too Shall Pass"

claims your landlord's tattoo, but waking
with your heart beating in my bicep
and my arm about to die
beneath you, I remember Esther
my old piano teacher, whose eyes
last time I saw her had long
forgotten light, but always knew where
Olin stood before he spoke: whose hands
so long curled to the keyboard somehow knew
where to grasp when he held out his
thin old arm to her— and wonder
if she felt the metronome inside him,
steady and familiar, wonder
if she heard our thousand clumsy fingers
waltzing on through the world without her?

Wheels in Love

This highway spans the time zones,
scissors the state line,
hurdles the river on steel and mathematics
but shies in a calculated curve
from the sea—
                         It is the male's
long abstraction of the search for sex.
It gives endless narrow room
for the broad-shouldered pride of the race.
It intersects other roads mostly
at right angles, with a wary circling.
It carries the lover of velocity almost clear
of his line and plane, almost to climax
in its steady convergence of asphalt and sky

(but every hilltop he conquers
lets him down)

                         This car
tracks the highway through the eye and arm
of the autonomous human male,
shielding him from the little deaths of insects,
the poison of his exhalation—

It is a mechanical model
of the intricate male ego, life-size.
It suspends every destination
from the spark and explosion of destiny confined.
It sings that deep single note
of any disappointed lover of the wind.
It blueprints his days and weeks and years
in a system of interlocking circles
which weekends he can dismantle and master

*(but every month his payment
comes around)*

Woman?
What do you think he keeps glancing up
to his rear-view mirror for?

Wolves Mate for Life

Wolves mate for life
What we call *love* is a striving
after them across the snowplain
of a queen-size sheet

And rare it is that two of us travel
in the same set of footprints for long

The spider is a good neighbor
What we call *heartbreak* is a starving
while we lie webbed in memory,
food preserved for ourselves, if we live

Till we remember whose spittle spun
the nightmare and yawn free

The birds trust their eggs lightly
to the high, thin branch
Tossed by windy longings we trust
first in our solitude, only later
in the longing of another

Strand by strand we weave a device
for living high in the air

Beggar's Lice

I have kept everything
she gave me, I still
take my hair out of the ponytail
before I sleep

                    I look
at every woman I admire
with the look she taught me,
fingering for luck
the semiprecious stone of her reply

I keep
the good nights like useless old coins
and spend them
on my rare overcast occasions
like so many moons

                    and I miss her
only when I climb this hill
to gather all the sun's
long fine hair in my hands
and kiss the lolling hip of the hills
across my hollow at sunset—

(Coming home
I find I've gathered only these
                    small seeds
called beggar's lice)

Umbilicus

for Dawn Aura

But in the end
we can only sing so much
loneliness

Yes, I came too from the planet
of the Siamese twins
separated before birth, each
fingering in secret the button
beneath our clothes, that old
scar under the skin,
remembering the place we were cut free
of one another

> *Like a starving man*
> *at the wedding reception,*
> *keeping an eye on the subsiding feast*
> *continually replenished,*
> *I fall in love all day with glimpses*
> *of the Goddess on the sidewalk,*
> *on the train—*

o

It is awesome
that we have grown to be this crowd
you might meet anyone in

I ride the subway like a surfer, slantwise
across the wave of five o'clock

And I think there is no end
to the beautiful tunes
spilling out of all these radio headsets

Around me the languages of the earth
ripple together like mingled rivers

And the one chewing gum,
she might be the one
I came this way to meet

o

No, beauty is instinct,
          inborn as breathing

Only vanity is skin-deep

her very collarbone a
                    sexual intelligence
beneath her skin

Heartache is in the eye
          of the beholder

trinkets at her ears
          the least and only lasting
piece of her

Such a burden it must be
          to be beautiful,
to resent the necessity
of ignoring me,
                    tossing her
translucent curls
against the spiderthread
I hold her by
                    just watching

and she never even
          had to learn
when to look so exquisitely
away

o

Someone is walking around
in the beat of my pulse all day.
Someone sleeps
in the marrow of my skeleton as I lie awake,
listening to my own eardrums.
Somebody breathes out whenever I
                                    breathe in.
Someone is traveling through time
to meet me, woman of a particular freckle
and fingerprint; we'll dance
back and forth between the telepathic look
and the intoxicated gland, the smoke
of philosophy and the spice of perspiration , , ,

Even my silence is full of pauses
                            listening for you!

o

Our first night together,
and she sleeps somewhere else . . .

Now if this globe was a theater
you would wake this morning to find me
mad on your balcony, spouting spontaneous
pentameter, as if roses were roses—
Well, true, I didn't seem to have any
sleep at all in me last night, the gulf
of constellations turning in my head, I kept
remembering your fingertips—
And I did keep up a fairly mad,
fairly regular blather of poetry,
rose-petals showering down like snow
from the dark, disappearing
at the click of the light leaving only
the list of their names in my hand, names
of things that don't need naming
to scent your breathing—

o

the sunshine later
dangles on a gold chain
against her throat

It's never the same
after you have touched someone
in a dark bed
                        Turning out that light
you step across the deep
chasm between two daylights
and daylight never looks the same again

                (impossible
        to clasp the old love back again
                now that the bone of my elbow
        knows your cheekbone)
                                        Breath
comes and goes, bearing three small
shuddering sobs and the weight
of the dark

                        o

        I guess I've cast some shadows your way
        I see you've used them under your eyes
        the way I spread your kisses on my lips
        for balm against the winter

        Last time we met your eyes were darker
        than the sky above the lake, your
        lashes iced as if you'd walked there
        in the wind's eye, weeping

        The sky was bright above the city
        A dark tide was receding at my temples
        Each glance you gave was an eclipse
        of all the stars and all but a strand or two
        of moon
                        (Later that night I found my first
        grey hairs in the mirror of a strange house)

Round and round the dancers
stamped and swung,
stamped and swung:
every so many measures
you spun back to me.
I tried hard
not to make metaphors of fact.
Your thin, fearless back
leaned out against my open hand
as we whirled our partners
again, again,
riding the centrifuge of 4:4 time,
safe in the grip of our
trust in gravity—

I feel
the muscles of your belly
flex
against my open hand
as you lift yourself
to the receiver of the phone
The tip
of my longest finger
finds your dimpled navel
and I feel your voice
vibrating through my whole hand
from
the sinews of your throat
down to your taut gut
as slung wires somewhere
hum
the little melody you sing each time
you speak

Why does the full moon
looming low and pale

on the rising twilight
remind me of you tonight?

Because underneath its silk
pajamas it too is
a bony lover, far from me.

Because it too brims with
mysterious light, and
nothing is between us but that
shining tide.

Because the cold waves rising
against my spine this
moment sing: *asphalt* and *steel*
while the moon casts a faint
dust of the other world down,
singing *crickets*

pine-smell

Because tonight we share
at least the same fool moon.

o

Two cups of coffee at midnight,
and she's wide awake when I tiptoe in

Eyes like the eyes of a small
startled animal shine from the dark,
faintly illuminating
that smile she has carried since she was a girl
just for tonight

A woman is made
to lie under a man, you told me once.
I like it better the other way around.

Lying here now we have outlived
our hunger, our need to speak,
all augury and remembering.
I am the flattened grass
where the doe has rested.
              You are
the branch still quivering
with the blackbird's departure.

          o

Of course you'd know that when I found her
        she'd be beautiful.
Worth growing up the rest of the way.

You wouldn't know her secret scars and
        invisible tattoos
like you know mine, friends, but
you can trust me to recognize them.

How else would I have known her?

Now that I have made her cry
and made her yell at me, she seems to have
        decided.
I'm the one born under her constellation
        of signs
returning to spawn, swimming in with the tide
as her river arrives
        and arrives.

She's made me suffer the subtle needle
        of her distress.
I wear the print of her teeth in my ear.
I too have made up my mind:
        she's the one
standing by the highway at first light
        with my unknown
destination crayoned on her sign.

Roadside Psalm

When the names
    are gone from the earth,
when the boundaries are lost in flowers
    and the signs fall soundlessly
    to either side,

when the trees send their children out
    into the meadows
    where our subdivisions crumble
and this highway washes down
    to silt the sea,

still your breath
    will stir the pine boughs
    over me
and the star in your eye
    will warm the stone that carries on
    my name

Here I lie
disintegrating under your touch
    Turn over, love
and touch me again

IV

TO THE
ENEMY
DEAD

Broken Wings & Artificial Flowers

1936. July. While the Falangists were
         occupying Granada, Federico Garcia
         Lorca was executed and his body
         thrown into an unmarked grave.

The birds are dead.

The flowers are out of a job.

Another poet
has disappeared into the ground.

The janitors are busy
scrubbing his elegies from the toilet stalls
of San Salvador and Cape Town,
the streetcleaners are sweeping up
his ballads among the crowd
at Tiananmen Square
while the politicians gesture
into dead microphones—

But the sky over Washington is white with feathers
falling, drifts of petals
will bury the avenues by nightfall
and the dead poet speaks
in that clearest of inks that runs
from the eyes
of women in mourning

Eyes of the Assassin

Animals die
in their ordinary clothes,
abandon their families
to the claws and teeth of time.
In whatever place
time has tracked them to
they turn and look—

In the eyes
of the hardened assassin,
a farmer sees his boy playing soldier
carrying the gun borrowed
with promises
from a dying compañero.
A nursing student sees the baby
she delivered that morning
hungrily grasping at air with tiny hands,
tiny lungs.
A brickmason sees his wife
bending with a bundle of twigs to light
the fire for breakfast,
black hair hanging,
sudden flame.
A schoolteacher sees her old father
smoking, the spot of blood
in his handkerchief,
his wallet full of pictures of the dead.

People lie
like animals in shabby clothes
along the highways. In their eyes
the animal fear has glazed
and dried, and a further look
distracts them: a rapture of release
into the twilight and the weeds.

The Price of Vigilance

I still walk the hot coals
of that smoky countryside some nights,
ankle-deep through villages
that will cool and blow away by morning,
down the hardening tracks of ox-carts
that have burdened one more
rutted road with the abandoning
of ancestors

Maps are changed in military
                              intelligences
and the feet in my jungle boots
are numb

                              I stand sentry
other nights over the long black wall
that names our dead, stamping
for warmth on the cold stone thinking
cold stone always makes the best monument
while a shiver somewhere
in my ribboned uniform stamps instead
at the smolder of a slow cremation
in the blood

Red flags flicker over that country
                              in memorial
to a harvest of ash from the mud fields
we waded

                    I marched once
in the Veterans Day parade
down the avenue between the marble buildings
on my hard rubber wheels
under banners hanging limp on the air,
under the confetti of lies
drifting from the P.A.

While my feet were still exploding
                        like phosphorus
in the white-hot hotel room where I
woke that morning

Taste the Fire

Close your eyes and bite down
into your lip. Bite deeply,
carefully, taste the wound's
salt agony with love: *This is your brother.*
This is the tide that rises
ceaselessly in the mouths
of nameless detainees who refuse to repent
of their poverty. *This is your sister.*
This is the river that flows
continuously from the beginning
of the memory of pain.
Taste the fire: we pass it on, welt
for welt, bruise for bruise,
till the smallest child has received the mark
of the innoculation. *Give the boy*
his own gun. Give the girl
her own mirror. Now
try to feel any pain but your own.

Cousin Who Would Fly
a Bomber for
the Sake of Flying,

I would rather see you dance
for nickels on the subway platform
than fly that blind furrow down
a blood-red radar field carrying seeds of fire

Lights on the instrument panel say
NOW which in the relativity
of motion means HERE, and you
close the lever that releases the bombs
while below ...

Cousin,
you have told me how you leap
to a perfect stillness in yourself
when you go dancing, how you feel
the constellations wheel about your breathing

Lights below in the darkness
blink out at the rumor of your approach,
families crowd into the shelters
while the village sentries watch the stars
for a shadow ...

Cousin,
I would rather see you dance
around your old army cap on the corner
than fly that dark trajectory down
the valley of your own shadow, reaping fire

Bombs fly their almost predictable curve,
strapped in your cockpit you fall with them,
watching as the computer tracks your success
you plunge to earth already miles behind the fire
of your jets...

Cousin,
you can fly from the toes of your old
sneakers if you close your eyes and fall
into that perfect darkness inside
where the blood and breath circulate and return

Buildings bloom behind you and collapse,
blood and breath escape their vessels,
your thunder silences the mouths of the survivors
and the village burns like a signal fire
signifying darkness...

Cousin,
I would rather see you dance
for drinks in some subterranean bar
than fly that tunnel of sky between stars
and the scattered constellations of your
unknown cousins

I would rather see you dance

54

The Money Missing from our Paychecks

We who eat
lest we grow hungry, we who
lie down to sleep
because we know to the minute
what time we rise,
                    a bomber is blinking
across our bathroom mirrors that does not sleep,
a sentry walks the perimeter of our dim bedrooms
till the alarm rings
and we reach out to stop it

A truckload of soldiers comes leaping out
into smoke and noise when we
tear open our paychecks every Friday in the bar,
a bomb drops away from the black wing
even while we curse
with ritual laughter the government
which has siphoned our blood in the night again
to fuel helicopters and tanks

A distant flame is casting those faint shadows
on the T.V. screen, a burning
that does not stop for Happy Hour,
while the bodies untangle from the pileup
and the referee bends to retrieve a fumble,
the family scattered
by an American bomb does not get up

The bodies are brown
as the football
waiting at the scrimmage line again, but broken
like the field they farmed

They are too busy giving their
blood back to the soil
to blame us, but it is our slow suffocation they fight
for every breath, the money missing
from our paychecks every Friday has bought us
the pumping of their hearts
to dip our chips in and wash down
with our beer

It is our war
and only our waking hands can reach out
to stop it

Duties of the Witness

But if the reports are true,
if it is our dollar bills that hire
squads of soldiers without uniforms
to perform the unctions
of the dead each night on someone
chosen from the living?

The price of democracy.

Is it not the duty
of those with imagination
to try to imagine how this must feel?

Our junior bureaucrats
that ship out the crates of cattleprods
and automatic rifle-clips each day,
every bullet "MADE IN U.S.A."—

The tools of vigilance.

Is it not the duty
of those with understanding
to try to understand where this must lead?

To the Enemy Dead

And how can I recognize my enemy
        if I turn down my television set?

—men in jungle colors moving
        against the jungle,
their guns attentive before them
        parting the twilight
as if to divide everything that is (that is
        anything that moves)
        in two

        How can I wish them well, how
can I wish them worse?

        —that one, him, slouching
unaffectedly for the cameras,
        stepping warily over the burial ground
of empires of brown people
        into the rifled barrel of the night
—my wish tumbling south like a random bullet
        dividing the air,
intersecting the sweat and tension of some (his
        or his enemy's)
        smooth young belly

        To live under the stench
of silence, of funeral speeches
        clenched in the fist,
of libraries of held breath—

Sometimes a silent man must
lift the rifle from the table, counting his rosary
     of ammunition
while his elder relatives make their crosses
     —and one night
his children wake to a distant fiesta, firecrackers
     from the mountains (dried peas
rattling in the pod—) the scattered shots
     like black seeds
     falling into silence

To live on and never see
the body of your lover, bury him under
     the pause in conversation,
a tower without bells—

Sometimes it matters
which way a man was looking when the darkness
     splintered his jaw
Sometimes it matters which way he was
     moving when he fell
Sometimes it matters most what the hope was as it is
     evaporating
     from his eye

And sometimes it matters
where my eye wanders during the commercial,
     whether I notice
who's bringing me the news

(Next, the report on our
newly-appointed ambassador to a nation
     we have hired mercenaries sworn
     to uproot from its dirt)

Sometimes, all
     of a sudden, something
     matters

Neruda's Drum

When Neruda died
the volcanoes shuddered like a spine,
an eagle wounded by its prey, but did not
shed a single steaming tear

> *The people walked in black lines*
> *on the mountainside, down the old paths*
> *of the generations of raindrops*
> *looking for a river*

The ocean stalked the long coast
like a tide of lions grinding sand in their jaws,
but did not cry out

> *The people wailed against*
> *the dark mouth that eats their passionate language*
> *voice by voice*

The wind kept up a grieving
that tore at the houses
as the dead tongue had torn at the heart,
but the houses did not fall

> *The people went home*
> *after the procession*
> *and Neruda's drum began to beat again*
> *slow*
> > *and certain*

V

NICARAGUA
LIBRÉ
FULL MOON

In Solidaridad con en pueblo de Nicaragua …

For ten days in December of 1989, I lived with a Nicaraguan family in a barrio *in Managua, part of a church-sponsored project to help the community build its first school. The country was decorated for an election, and devastated by my government's ten-year covert war and economic embargo against the Sandinista Revolution. With a group of two dozen* norteamericanos *I visited a wide range of places in and around the city, listening to people on all sides of the struggle for Nicaragua's soul.*

Halfway through our visit, six days before Christmas, the United States invaded Panama. We joined a crowd of thousands outside our own Embassy to protest, only a few days after our interview with a staff member there. In the Nicaraguan papers and news broadcasts we saw image after image of an indiscriminate destruction that was eerily absent from the U.S. media on our return.

Two months later the Nicaraguan people voted the Sandinistas and their health care, literacy and land reforms out of office. The opposition party, UNO, won with the help of a multi-million dollar campaign contribution from the U.S. Congress— and the U.S. President's teasing promise of peace and plenty.

Everywhere we went in Nicaragua we heard the commitment to independence and the cry for peace. The cry for peace won out. The fighting has subsided now, but peace has not come. The real war goes on. Nicaragua is not free.

But once a people get in the habit of elections, I imagine, elections will keep coming around. It is with great respect and faith in the future of the Nicaraguan people that I dedicate to them this poem.

And with a prayer for the conscience of my own country.

Nicaragua Libré Full Moon

Augusto C. Sandino International Airport.

The same full moon I saw
>   fading
over the runway at O'Hare this morning
rising young and strong
over the airport palms at twilight:
>   full circle.

A committee from the *barrio* is here to greet us.

> *"Don't be afraid. Before anyone could*
> *touch your body, they would have to pass*
> *over the corpses of our bodies."*

> (How can I stand
> on a ground
> matted with the fallen hands
> of the trees? Comfortably.
> But when I notice the faces
> covered by those fingers,
> the eyes peering through
> every crack in the forest floor . . .)

Barrio Arnoldo Real Espinosa, Managua.

> Gather it all in:
> noises of the *barrio* before dawn,
> bare feet in the dirt,
> dogs with those perpetual
> grins on their faces, toilet seat
> leaning on the wall by the john—

> *Start with the premise that*
> *everyone loves*

The hook of his elbow caught
and lifted our bag off its wheels, swung it
across the sawdust and cement
of the living room floor. The elbow with no hand.
I felt those tiny wheels when they
touched down again, bearing that honor, that
shame.

She slept on a pallet in the corner of that
concrete slab. I lay listening
through her pillow in the master bedroom,
sweating through my sheets into her best mattress.
A parrot with opinions. Then roosters
and the radio in the black pre-dawn. In the morning
the sawdust was swept and gone, her living room
immaculate.

> *Start with the premise that everybody hurts*
> *who loves*

I came here to learn what I
already knew:
people live here. Each one has a name.
They have eyelashes and fingernails.
They drink beer and go to church.
They laugh with the laughtrack on T.V., each
in a different voice.
They decorate the house for the holidays.

They have faces. A few bear
the scars of the science of torture.
A few still look out from their solitary cells.
The rest bear the sign
etched in their foreheads
of unforgettable remembering.

> (Yes, they have barbershops.)

Jot this down, another
glimpse: handcart and bulldozer,
Santas in every nativity scene,
a homemade Ferris wheel
of patio chairs, blowing horns and
speed bumps, "policemen lying down—"

"This land was to be a park.
Due to the need we asked the city
to give it for a school."

I wore my calluses off
swinging this shovel down in a hole,
pala, poking with a chisel-pointed *bara*
to loosen the soft dark soil
for *la escuela*

(Where we piled dirt, a scooped-out hollow:
the kids are helping us again.
One pushing each arm of the wheelbarrow,
at least one riding every load—)

The foreman comes by at last,
hooks his Soviet fishing line to its nail
across my hole, drops his measuring stick
to the scraped clay floor. He nods, no smile—
but that evening when I go by,
this school has a corner: concrete post,
the reinforcing steel we cut, the wires
we twisted

(Workmen watching the ball game
over their shoulders, setting
another pre-fab concrete pillar in its hole
just outside the base path
at the broken cinderblock of second base

—the builder's apprentices
not so long ago players in that game . . .)

> *"When one of our sons dies, the mother says*
> *'My son lives.' But where does he live?*
> *He lives in the place where he spoke and people listened.*
> *Perhaps now there is a school there—*
> *that is where he lives."*

Afternoon Interviews.

> Take it home for a souvenir:
> masking tape instead of
> adhesive in surgery, no spare parts
> for the fluoroscope and x-ray
> made in the U.S.A., adult-size
> I.V. needles even for the kids—

In the mornings we build a school.
In the afternoons we are students
ready with our pens, scribbling
out the blood of the spilled hearts
of ten years (all the centuries of warfare—)

> *"It is sad to die, but even more sad to die forever."*

> *"They burned our houses and they*
> *burned everything we owned."*

> *"You can't condemn someone for their past until they die."*

> *"There have been errors and mistakes.*
> *But the government hasn't tried to hide them.*
> *It has confessed to the people,*
> *'Here we were wrong. But let's go ahead.'"*

> *"There is not a chemically pure Revolution."*

(Some of the most poetic words
I've ever heard
come out of the mouths of translators of Spanish.)

"It was hard to leave the city. We had the memory
in our hearts of all the people who had died."

That universal gesture, handing one
cigarette across to light the other—
these injured war veterans from El Salvador
could be any huddle of teenage
football heroes . . .

"Death squads walked down the street
just like a soccer team might, with guns."

They've just had a different
education.

Mothers of the Heroes and Martyrs, Matagalpa.

File the images away: grass
growing on the telephone wires
and clay tile roofs, water hurrying in its
irrigation ditch under the highway,
oxcarts full of firewood, windmill
turning under the first of the stars—

"When my son died I closed myself
in my house and would not come out."

The Mothers' meeting house:
a cement floor, framed two-by-fours,
a corrugated tin roof look like
they've always been here.
(But I remember the bare ground
that birthed a school: I imagine the day
they swung hammers, poured cement
and made it real)

Sing, laugh, cry, dance:

"Can there be more pain that one
can suffer than to lose a son?"

Yes, reply the mothers of the kidnapped
who still don't know

(100,000 mothers understand
who still pay interest on the cost
of Vietnam)

"I am proud now as if you were my own children."

You disappointed idealists
are a plague on the world
If the people don't rule
the way Democracy requires,
line them up and
even down the numbers a little

"He is of the dead that never die."

ON THE BUS TO THE BEACH.

Point your camera through the glass:
ruin of the *hacienda*, cactus pillars
still standing, cross on the church,
radio tower on the mountain,
roadside gravemarker
by the speed-limit sign—

This countryside keeps
pulling my eyes from poetry,
drowning the letters in green:

wild mountains and the hollows of corn,
shadows plunging down the hill,
sunlight lifted on rearing grasses,
vulture scooping out the mountainside
on its wings, jungle climbing on
roots and flowers to the sky's blue crags—

"We as Nicaraguans want to make our own history."

and the road all the while
tracking the telephone wires
on their concrete poles to the sea

"I thank God you have not abandoned us and left us alone."

We are almost alone on the beach:
a resort barren of *turistas.*
They have receded like a tide that never returned.
The waiters at the hotel,
kids selling necklaces of shells,
the thatched umbrellas
each dropping a well of shadow on the hot sand

and the insomniac sea
playing its never-tiring game with the beach—

"We're always here struggling . . ."

La Plaza de la Revolucion.

Play the game, bargain them down:
a coin worth less than its
metal, bright red, yellow, green
in the market poised for rotting,
the boneyard of automobiles, *"Pluma,
la pluma!"* a child begging for my pen—

The artist employed: girl with a paintbrush
and headphones, filling in the lines
of her lettering—

En la Tierra Paz

—working into the evening on a life-size
Christmas creche under a round-pillared
stone pavilion

while a drowsy soldier leans
on the muzzle of a rifle slung from his own neck

"Christ was a man like we are— suffered like we do—"

Across the plaza
a broken-haloed saint holds one end of a banner:
Daniel Presidente Vota por FSLN

> *"Although we were believers, in those days*
> *we felt scared going out alone…"*

Cathedral open to the sky,
a mass of weeds between thick columns
under the rusty skeleton of a roof,
mosaics and frescoes and saints
ascended into stone:
above the altar a dove
with no head
perpetually alighting—

> *"Jesus too was killed for being on the side of the poor."*

People come to sit
high on the ruined ledges,
gaze down from the balconies
across the *Plaza de la Revolucion*
into the evening

> *"Russians are atheists; they eat their kids.*
> *They make soap out of their old folk.*
> *But they give us bread. The North Americans*
> *send us missionaries to teach us of God.*
> *But the evil Commies send us bread."*

DEC. 19, 1989: STILL AVENGING CUSTER

> Remember how far from
> home you are— stickball in a dirt alley
> under overhanging trees,
> *Star Trek* in Spanish, Prince
> and Michael Jackson commercials
> in that idiom of synthesizers and hips—

On the morning after the U.S. invaded Panama,
my host mother washed my dirty jeans.
I hadn't asked her to.
(Had timidly tried scrubbing one
dirty t-shirt against the concrete washboard
in her sink—)
She hung them out in her courtyard
on a barbed-wire clothesline.

In another house a grandmother told the news
and then clasped herself in her own arms, all
goosebumps (she has had
no men at all in her family since the Revolution):
"I'm so cold," she said. *"I'm so cold."*

> *"We must forgive the Marines. They are used.*
> *Can you imagine what kind of Merry Christmas*
> *25 families will have when they receive their 25*
> *corpses?"*

Today Roberto our schoolteacher and our mayor Miguel
are dressed up as soldiers.
Last night at midnight, soldiers were
leaping out of airplanes into empty space,
the unknown new decade's dark
pre-dawn—

> (This is the future swaying
> dim below us as we dangle
> under our parachutes, seeds of our
> forefathers' sins drifting down
> on the zodiac of streetlights—)

But
the Panamanian defenders had quietly left town
an hour before midnight,
and the bombs are in full bloom
in the streets of Panama City this morning

falling at random
like those telegrams announcing
you have just won the sweepstakes

> *And the angel marked*
> *the houses of the faithful*
> *so that death might pass over*

> (Heat-seeking missiles only know
> one code, the B-52s
> only follow orders)

And the nuns in the convent
caught between war zones spend the day
prostrate on the floor

> *American bombs fall*
> *on the unjust as on the just,*
> *and the Prince of Peace*
> *returns this year in clouds of gore*

It's Christmastime
The marketing computers are busy
dividing up the territory
The North Americans are crowding
into lofty malls to worship
All over Latin America families gather around radios
spouting urgent Spanish into the cooling night

> (This morning 150 civilian deaths
> estimated in Panama: still
> avenging Custer)

and on the Voice of America the President says

> *"We went in with maximum force*
> *to ensure mimimal civilian casualties*

> *No numbers, can't help you there*
> *The hospital reports are unconfirmed—"*

(A language must do many things:
advertise the college of beauty,
spit slogans on the cemetery wall,
turn the speechwriter's trick

But once in a while it is called on
to serve in the emergency telegram,
in the grief of a priest, in the transport
of the radio commentator—)

and the Panamanian ambassador says

*"We were your friends,
the best friends you had in Central America . . ."*

The tank is a filthy creature
When one after another goes clattering past
over the Somoza brick,
the air grows foul with their exhaust

(On their way to surround our Embassy,
we found out next morning—
crouched behind its double fence, twin
coils of barbed wire blazing
like electric filaments in the sun . . .)

It's been too long
since the shelling of Vicksburg,
since the British burned Washington,
too long already since Vietnam

*"To go out glorified with your equipment and backpack,
come back injured or dead . . .
They are manipulated by a system.
They are also our brothers."*

Because we have forgotten who
we were, because we do not notice
what we have become,

the coffee comes dirt cheap this morning,
the dirt is dark with the drained
courage of corpses
and hardly anything is as profitable
as selling Coca Cola in a hot country

> *It is not possible to live on both sides*
> *of that line.*
> *Now I have told you:*
> *taking one more breath is taking*
> *sides.*

All modesty of poets is
false modesty: I speak for the sunspots
and the larvae of fireflies. I speak for the icecaps
and the vapor of teardrops. I speak for the volcano
lying awake under the waning moon and I speak
for the patient remembering of the poor.

> *"… the attempt to invade Nicaragua*
> *would be the biggest mistake the U.S. ever made."*

We don't see many smiles today
except for the children, thank God,
the children always smile

> *"A surgical strike"*
> —the phrase rings in every
> stroke of the pick, down here
> in my hole
> We dig
> trenches for the other war

> *To bury this country*
> *they'll have to uproot these concrete*
> *columns we have sunk into*
> *dark beautiful dirt and clay*
> *the many colors of these*
> *children*

VI

NOT ONE OF US
WILL ESCAPE
THE RAPTURE

Déjà Vu,
New Year's Eve

Who's to say
whether this particular
point in our
journey together around the sun
marks any significance
in the vast circumference of things,
but it's 11:44 of the 365th day
since we were all
here before

A hundred years ago
the ghost dance warriors died in the snow
at Wounded Knee
Their blood flowed
with the creek water, mingled
with the topsoil of a broken territory,
riding the muddy
river down to salt the sea

An invisible wave is
crossing the dark Atlantic,
dividing the globe,
a theoretical curve is
crashing over Times Square
and neon flares on
television screens all the way
to the Pacific—

Junebug

A junebug landed on his head, and he could see:
he felt the clasping tiny claws,
the buzz of wings between his eyebrows as
the six legs hugged him, hard,
just above the bridge of his nose—
place known variously as sixth chakra,
center of intellect and will
or third eye, sensing-organ of delight—

And not five minutes ago he had edged to the door
with that same junebug on his leg,
or its impostor, but lost it
somewhere on the way: this time, lumbering
crosseyed across the carpet,
he made it out the door and somehow
flung the thing away.

But love or loyalty
or hunger, dumb intuition, some old
locust will, vast insect wisdom— Christ,
he thinks, stands gulping down the air:
the junebug, crawling up his forehead to the seventh
or crown chakra, thousand-petalled lotus,
gateway to divinity that completes
the human mass-to-energy equation—

The junebug flew from the top of his head
to his raised fingertip: he regarded it
by starlight, grasped it gently, drew back
and tossed it to the stars.

Cover the Dead

> *Cover the dead*
> *first*
> *with some sort of sheet*

The highest point in Illinois
was heaped there by human tools,
basket after basket
of the living soil:
a long green mound along the bank
of the Mississippi.

> *Cover them next*
> *in makeup and their best*
> *clothes*
> *or better*

Human tools built the world's
tallest building on the lake
of the Illinois:
black steel girders and dark glass,
fitted marble along a sidewalk
where homeless people pass all night
in no particular
> hurry—

> *Cover them again*
> *with some glazed planks*
> *cut*
> *skillfully at the corners*

No one knows who heaped this hill
or why: they may have caverned their dead
in monuments of earth,
curled like fetuses asleep for the duration
of the journey between worlds—

                              (But who

could have buried them in turn,
those ancient basket-weavers
and earth-movers?)

> *Then cover the planks*
> *with a galvanized steel shell*
> *guaranteed*
> *for the life of the purchaser*
> *or better*

We embalm our living
in fluorescent light under monuments
of debt. They hurtle
through our netherworld in carriages
of steel and glass, sitting alone,
swaying together for the long journey home
in no particular
                    direction—

> *Cover the steel with dirt*
> *by the handful*
> *and the backhoe-load*
> *and cover the dirt finally*
> *with flowers and sod*

                              (But who will

bury us when our turn comes,
a black night over everything?
Who will
cover our dead?)

The Attorney for Death

I met the attorney for death out running
          on the beach,
his footfalls matched mine so well
          I didn't know he was behind me
till he drew alongside

He grinned through his dark glasses and
              offered me a cigarette
"Don't smoke 'em," I panted, he said
          neither did he and laughed out loud

He seemed to be gaining on me the whole time
          we held stride for stride

A beeper yelped at his hip and he answered,
ordering the buying and selling of orphanages
              and graveyards
named for certain living villages I know well

The washing of the waves gave voice to the
              ancient cavern in me,
deep shadow I can swim to in a cold breath,
eyes closed, though it's
          too dark down there anyhow to see

          His breathing was light,
his strides graceful and athletic as the old
          gods must have been

The sun hissed in liquid metal
              on the horizon
He cast a chill on me as he went past

              though he threw no shadow

"I am thinking about the enemy gods,
    the enemy gods, among their weapons now
    I wander.
Ay-ye-ye-ye-ya-hai!
Now Slayer of Enemy Gods, I go down alone
    among them . . ."

Navaho war song

All the Umbrellas! All the Balloons!

The five poems that follow are pieces of a sequence on nuclear war. After the Soviet Union had dropped out of the arms race and the U.S. had shut down all its nuclear weapon plants for safety violations, I put the poems away for a time, presuming that nuclear war was one danger we were mercifully spared.

But the United States continues to build the first-strike Trident missile system. We continue to test new weapons in the Nevada desert, homeland of the Western Shoshone Nation. The government is pressing ahead with plans for a new generation of nuclear weapons. The danger of a nuclear accident remains with us; so does the 50-year accumulation of top secret, unregulated radio-active waste. Pluto-nium contaminates every mother's milk.

I have come to doubt the sanity of my country's leaders. Who is it they fear so deeply? Who is safe from such a lust for dominance? Spending our wealth on such dark visions for so long is sapping our nation of its strength. With or without a nuclear war, I begin to see, the quest for nuclear supremacy will ruin us as surely as it has our "enemy."

And if the people of this country do not recognize their true enemy in time— war itself— these poems may yet prove prophetic.

Submarine

Eating the thin-sliced
and delicately curled flesh
    of an animal
with shredded lettuce on
the thick slices of good bread

I think of the submarine
that rises like a shadow
under our children's
    faces as they sleep

and of the shadows of clouds
    I have watched
skimming the dry harvest
of the hills, travelling
the westward surge of rangeland
where the cattle stand
shouldering the wind together
    —sunlight
on the bottom of a stream

and moon-glimmer
at the bottom of a barren sea,
a silted ruin
    full of treasures
that was a child's room once

I still sleep there sometimes
when I lie awake
    with too much food
fingering the bones inside my wrist,
wondering if I'll find a wife
in time

On the 'B' Train

The train goes down into its tunnel.
Sound ceases in the lighted cars as we plunge
into the ricochet of wheels on rails,
gazing out through our faces in the dark glass.

TRICK OR TREAT SLAYER SOUGHT

*Far out on the ocean
the submarine is surfacing,
water streaming down black flanks.
A steel hatch is rolling on steel
runners in the forward deck. The nose
of the missile catches the first glint of the day.*

IT'S NOT EASY BEING A PARENT
Are Your Kids Getting to You?

At each subterranean station
shoals of passengers commingle and dissolve:
in the pause between silences a baby cries.
A boy in a neck brace presses close to his mama.

MORE THAN A GREAT NATIONAL BESTSELLER
A Great Way of Looking at Life

*Schools of porpoises leap
in the dawn glare as a thousand tons
of pressurized steel ride the slow hill of each
enormous wave. Down in the dim hull
grave men study lighted screens.
Overhead the last pale stars are winking.*

"NO SMOKING, LITTERING, OR PLAYING
OF MUSICAL INSTRUMENTS ON THE TRAIN!"

So five young girls practice harmonies.
Two kids in spiked hair and leather lean together
on a steel pole by the door. Lights flash
in the tunnel ahead, shooting fire down the rails.

Firestorm

The crowd was our only shelter

The wind above us was alive with fire

We ran all together for the bridge

The ground beneath us was alive
        with twisting torsos,
          hands grabbed at my ankles

We reached the river in a mass
          too large to cross

The water was alive with struggling
          faces, hands reaching
          from the fiery reflection of sky

There was not a sound anywhere

I gripped the hand of the woman beside me
          and we pressed toward the center

I squeezed past the pylon of the bridge
          but the crowd pinned her
          to the concrete

I freed my hand just in time

Those of us in front made the bridge
          just as another crowd burst
          between the pylons at the far end

Their eyes were alive with the fire
          behind us

They cried out in a strange language
          but among them I recognized
          each of my enemies

Ashes Fall at Christmas in Hell

Yes. This is ash.
Don't trust it in your vaccuum cleaner bag.
Sweep it gingerly from your rug,
dump the dustpan in a doubled plastic sack.
Carry the trash to the curb.
Let the masked men lift and heave,
let the big truck haul it
away.

Keep the kids in. Stay home tonight
and watch the cable. Don't watch the news.

Yes. Only smoke.
Keep walking, let it fall behind your shoulder.
It will settle with the snow.
Don't track any in; shrug it off like skin
at the door, cough it up
like the aftertaste of an abortion
and spit. Get rid of it
some way.

Seal the windowcracks and the chimney.
Tell the kids one last lie about the morning.

Yes. Fire.
Let it fall from your hand.
Crush the coals to cinder and damn the price
of the rug: flush away the shoe.
Wear the rubber gloves when you touch your
children. Touch them often. Don't listen
when they pray.

Kiss the kids goodnight now every night
for the last time. Wear your mask.

Every night is Christmas Eve in hell.

The Drummer at the Demonstration

October 13, 1984
Chicago

Under the microphone
my hands seem to know exactly which note
the twin taut skins should sing,
their bass and tenor voices call to this crowd
at rest after marching, dance!
but only one wet pair of feet is
answering—

From the bandshell stage
Grant Park is a rainbow of umbrellas and balloons.
The day around us is not large:
it is easy to imagine that we are America, crowded
here between Michigan Avenue
and the lake to celebrate a victory over wars
at last. Over one last
victory that would have left nothing but the spoils.

This mist we breathe
beneath our umbrellas
is fallout from the factories of Chicago,
our thin taut skins on sticks
would protect us better from the drumming
of a hard fall rain—

It is just as easy to imagine
that we are travellers on an ocean without harbors,
wondering if this time the water
will subside. Each race represented among the survivors.
Our leaders would have us hide
under an umbrella of flame! We send up balloons
to our enemies instead, filled
with wet songs and shouts and the breathing of children.

> *The gas inside these*
> *thin taut skins on strings*
> *seems to tug toward a common sun somewhere,*
> *it has lifted two or three more*
> *specimen drops of color high above the crowd*
> *every time I look—*

Russia lies under her huge night
on the other side of this soft mud skin drawn tight
between us. Her leaders
do not sleep well tonight, but in the featherbeds
of her millions it is birds,
not missiles, that rise in dense flocks over the pole
from the country they fear. Birds
carrying branches. Birds of every color in the rainbow.

> *I am only the drummer*
> *at the demonstration, but looking out*
> *from the bandshell stage I see*
> *the damp spangled banners tense on their poles*
> *and two dozen dancing pilgrim feet*
> *planting footprints in the mud of some just*
> *uncovered island—*

All the umbrellas! All the balloons!

Not One of Us
Will Escape the Rapture

I don't believe in heaven

No one will be famous any more

Any minute now
the television sets will all go blind,
whole families watching will glance up
through their picture windows,
noticing all at once the tempest of gases
steadily erupting into light
a million miles away

                            as people
passing a plate-glass storefront glance
into a brief secret self

We are only minor demons
in one another's hell

She moves on the screen with diabolical
                           grace

Down in the airconditioned
Inferno, where cigarette-tips burn red
and smoke rides the television's blue beam,
electronic drums sell the New
Army at halftime

                        The drinkers
disregard the moon at the window
looking in through the COLD BEER sign's cool fire
—one more replay of the tackle
that bent the runner's knee in two
directions

Never trust a famous face
she says with her eyes on me
above the crowd

                    Each poet
leads a private tour of purgatory

The schools are full of maps and clocks
and reconstructed skeletons,
bright dead leaves, volcanoes in blossom
on the bulletin board

                        Earthrise blooming
on the calendar by the door

And the children bent over their crayons,
the millenium so near they can taste it
on their pink protruding tongues

Any minute now
the stars will quake in the heavens

People will come rushing out of their houses
and fall back staring on the grass
as if this was the first sight
granted to the blind

                    In a twinkling
the galaxies begin the long return

Not one of us,
not the man bruised by weather
sleeping on the subway with two fingers gone,
not the newest baby born
already wounded, suffocating in hospital light,
not one of us will escape the Rapture

New Year

To be thwarted
by cold chance—
aborted
like the pinned hooves of a calf
that tried its best to be born
into the January weather
until it died,
like the splayed awkward legs of its mother
round and huge on her side
in the snow, torn
by tiny struggling hooves,
frozen beyond complaint of the cold
or the stiffness
of circumstance—

To be caught in the if-ness,
to be left half
unborn, half-delivered when you die only proves
you have touched the world
you reached for

It's a new year
Now then
reach again

VII

WHAT
WE
SHARE

A Hymn to the Mystery of Waking

*Buried workglove
reaching out of the grass . . .*

Whatever it is that makes my body
live, the cells
intelligent, whoever
makes this music in the brain,
I thank you

(I bequeath my fat to Gaia:
just let me keep a single
blues refrain!)

*Rusted jawbone of an old
rearview mirror smashed flat . . .*

Whoever it is
that lives in the touch of fingers,
whatever sings
that song our hands go on humming
when the circle breaks up,
we thank you

(We surrender all
our licenses and deeds to the earth:
just let us keep the smell
of one lover's juice!)

*Bees at work
inside a clear plastic
sack of garbage in the dumpster . . .*

Whatever it is
that fills the trees with first light
and the waking of birds,
whoever spilled
breaking day across the lake,
I'm grateful

(I offer my own waking
to the power that ravenously eats
the hours, just let me
recall this soaring vastness
between heartbeats—)

*I remember now, Spring
always comes again*

All the Precious Fungi

All the precious fungi of the earth
spring up between her toes
*we bury one another in the dark
of her eyes—*

Mother
who taught the mothers all their songs,
open your eyes again,
we bring one more child to be heaped
with those high starry spaces

Mother who feeds the songbirds
their bright berries,
sing through your trees the breath of rain
we lie listening for at night

and wake the spores of toadstools
underneath the leaves
you dropped in your slow-breathing
sleep

A Lantern on the Mountain

Apparition
from the hour before sleep:
mothership of the fireflies, a tipi
glowing like a lantern in the clearing—

> *(but the dark is as lovely*
> *as the light*
> > *and last night*
>
> *I only found my way home*
> *by the light of the fireflies)*

Only canvas
on crossed sticks, lit by my
solitary candle, decorating the only
piece of level ground in these parts—

> *(trees of a hundred human*
> *lifetimes ago,*
> > *a skin of moonlight*
>
> *in the night of no moon*
> *as if this is where she hides)*

Apparition
from the century before Columbus:
nautilus of the unborn, lantern for my
silence before the typewriter each morning—

> *(but the dark is always*
> *ancient*
> > *while the trees*
>
> *add one more ring, growing*
> *young in the spring again)*

Near the summit
of something huge and dark,
a resting place on this steep piece
of my life: a lantern on the mountain.

*To commemorate the 40th Hiroshima Day, 25,000 people came to Wash-
ington to tie a Ribbon of 18-inch segments around the Pentagon, across the
Potomac, around the Capitol and down the Mall to the Lincoln Memorial. Created
by peace groups, church groups, sewing circles, schoolchildren, families and
individuals around the world, each banner celebrated uniquely in patchwork,
needlework, batik, silkscreen, weaving, paint or collage "what I'd hate to lose in a
nuclear war." When our circle was complete, we tied them all together to create a
continuous Ribbon 18 miles long.*

The Ribbon

August 4, 1985

I. Eastbound

I wake up this morning climbing mountains
on the bus.
     Our highway
climbs the shadow of a hill, Pennsylvania
sprawled around us under its green patchwork,
hunched behind a sleeping shoulder

           against the sun—

*Underneath our seats we carry patches
of the dream of Illinois, a flat country far behind
where the eastbound blacktops have not yet waked:
among our luggage as we sleep
we carry pieces of a Ribbon rumored ten miles long.
We are bearers of the broken segments
of a circle.*

     Daybreak
bursts around us as we crest the rise. Another bus
has crept up in the outer lane, is passing,
sparks of sunrise flying between its wheels—
ILLINOIS, I read,
    THE RIBBON—

No one awake but the drivers and me.
Beneath my feet the bus is singing; around me
the choir of people climbing mountains
in their sleep.

II. At the Memorial

Late to the demonstration, and my God!
Didn't anyone even show up?
A couple hundred people clustered round the feet
of Lincoln—

I step over a Ribbon on the grass
and remember:
this isn't a demonstration. It's three points
striving to become a circle.
This gathering has stretched out arms
toward two others, bearing its
thousands of banners each on two feet.
These people resting here by the reflecting pool
are the procession.

Strolling the Ribbon it becomes difficult
to look up at all the eyes.
Once I do look up I see:
they are the Ribbon, and it grows difficult
to look down at the next banner. When I do
I see that all these banners
are the Ribbon after all.
These friendly and good-looking folks
are a parade: *the circus audience*
has left the stands and surrounded all three rings,
ladies and gentlemen,
demanding a turn in the lights—

Someone asks me to carry two banners.
I wear them as a cape
and watch Pete Seeger straining up to the mike,
scrawny under his guitar,
his voice a young man's voice again
above this crowd:
"You are the bearers of the Ribbon!"

We can see the end of the procession
reaching toward us now
across the reflection of sky in the pool.
The Pentagon and the Capitol are tied.
They need people
to stretch these heaps of banners out
to close the circle—

Mary Peifer, Illinois, I bear your banner.
Over two knots I made friends:
a woman who just arrived last night, my God,
by boat from Australia, bearing her banner,
a cabinetmaker in a yellow shirt
who's buying ground
not far from where we stand
to plant in. His banner came
from California—

           We stand
on the steps of the Memorial.
I tie a good square knot
and the three of us
join the circle.

And the Wind Fell Bleeding

for Martin Luther King, Jr.
January 20, 1986

How long has it been
since I cried three times
in a night?

Once at the newsreel
of the three cops in riot helmets
wrestling the portly grey-haired lady
down

      Again at the words
swelling in the golden throat of the dreamer
who saw the promised land and knew
we could not conquer it by killing
this time

      And again when I heard
how that windpipe shattered
and the wind fell bleeding

And I kept thinking what if
all over America in black
factory towns and cities
full of white marble
      people are
walking out of chapels
and capitol rotundas tonight
feeling what I feel?

Convergence

August 16, 1987
Chicago

We are each and all so much more
necessary than we know

A Japanese goldfish glowing in the sky
as we gather for sunrise,
Orion aiming his reliable bow,
the planet of the morning still bright
beyond the moon—

Surely the differences among us are
only for admiring

Shall we dance?
back and forth between the Sunday morning
traffic and the birds of dawn,
between our wishful rituals and these
unwilling fingers—

We're so much stronger when we just
hold hands

Peace could come
like a sifting snow some early
morning, ghostly at first
until it begins to gather in the cracks,
glisten in the sheltered places

Standing in our circle by the lake
we close our eyes and breathe the single
wish together—

Peace could come

The Name on my Cross

April 23, 1990
Fort Benning, Georgia

Juan Ramon Moreno S.J.,
I carried your cross
in the circular procession today,
shaking my rattle.

I confess
I leaned on your cross a little
during the speeches,
rattling my applause.
Then looked over my shoulder.

The soldiers stood
in little motionless groups
as if posing for photographs with their
personnel carriers,
in battle camouflage and riot gear.
They watched.
I couldn't tell if they listened.

I hoisted your cross
and turned your name around to face them.
Not to accuse anyone:
I wanted to feel the weight of the wood.
And I wanted them to notice
you had a name.
Not just another dark-skinned man on a cross.

*Father Moreno was one of six Jesuit priests killed by members of
the Salvadoran military on November 16, 1989. Five of the
soldiers convicted for his murder received training at the U.S.
Army School of the Americas at Ft. Benning. We'll know real
change is coming to El Salvador when they shut it down.*

What We Share

It's all real, of course

But what we share is
this earth
we stand on to see,
earth to our horizons,
earth in space
and space itself, our
individual darknesses
pierced
by lights

> *Not these flitting*
> *shadows in our heads, blind*
> *boundaries of nations*
> *no more real than the lines*
> *of the constellations*

But sometimes one
another,
as if by luck, strangers
breathing together
the mutual delusion
of the moment, linked
as long as the finger
touches
the drum

> *And nothing is more real*
> *than what the children will inherit,*
> *our love for the soil*
> *like a handful of tiny seeds cast*
> *to the springtime*

The notes leap from the hand,
vanishing, all
but what we share

Feather and Shadow

> *We have come to the time of the choosing
> of ancestors.*

This is the place where my ancestors came down
from their square hole in the sky

> *The world is
> bigger than we can see,* that
> long horizon promised.
> So they built ships.

My ancestors grew corn here, this is the clearing
where they danced the year

> Preparing to abandon
> their bodies, they built cathedrals
> where the ancient groves had been.
> *The world is bigger than we can see …*
> One by one the monks
> fell unconscious in their cells.

My ancestors camped here in the Winter
of the Early Snow, they knew the spot by the stars

> The unknown continent grew
> vaster as they conquered,
> the imaginary cities grew richer
> in their delirium: each
> Crusader, each Conquistador
> conjuring a private mansion,
> lying in his fever and his cloud of flies.

This is where the young men came
fasting and singing, alone in the sacred land

It might have been my great-grandfather
bending, the boy at the plow
too young to remember that horizon
of unbroken acreage, hanging back
against the pull of the mule
to pluck a flint-shard from the vanished prairie grass—

This is where my ancestors came
to honor their dead, this windy ridge in the sky

> *He looks up. Clouds break*
> *into feathers, streaking over*
> *the horizon. He sees one*
> *sweep across the sun and the bright land of his father falls*
> *into shadow.*

We have come to the time of the choosing

> *This is my native place.*
> *This mountain. This creek.*
> *This is my native place.*

Dragonfly's Song

Just rising
from the little spring
I stood looking
from the shoulder of the mountain—

> *Silence,*
> *and out of its mouth*
> *a dragonfly's song*
> *sings*

I came down from the mountain
carrying just what I carried up
and five pretty leaves.

Poet Working
the Dawn Shift Again

for Paul Goodman

I have taken sides.
A poet can no longer stand
in the yard at night alone
travelling the constellations
at the speed of darkness.
We have work to do inside.

Not enough to sing the dark
with the crickets, sing the moon
with a coyote, not enough
to stay up and sing dawn with the birds—

Song alone can't save us,
the thousands that parade for peace,
the millions that gather weekly to sing
to the Creator Spirit: song
alone can't save us from the blinding
of the sun and moon and stars.

Not enough to chant my ocean
through some seashell of a heart,
hum my love-song blossom to blossom
across the garden where my children sleep —

I have married my muse.
I have inherited a house of wind and light,
of acorns and root-hairs, hawk's feather,
turtleshell, cicada-skin:
the poetry of clasping hands
alone can save us, this language that leaps
at the speed of light from eye to eye.
That and the work.

If we have a chance of leaving earth
an inheritance to others as we received it,
what work is more worthwhile?
And if we fail, and die together,
what work is worth
anything at all?

Hindsight

The ones who
dig up the ground to make power,
they forget

whose power it is

The ones who use up
the ore in the rocks to make war,
they forget

where power comes from

We who sleep
in this soft place on the earth,
we remember

the debt we owe to gravity

We who sit
in council with the rocks and trees,
we remember

a stone guards every grave

Any place is powerful
where we choose to stand and give
our lives to the earth

The roots go down into the ground

ABOUT THE AUTHOR

Stephen Wing started thumbing his way to school when his bicycle was stolen in the middle of the 12th grade. Traveling by thumb was his undeclared major in college, and after graduating in 1978 he began twelve years of serious post-graduate wandering. He is the product of a missionary family, suburbia, canoeing in Quetico, the liberal arts, the American counterculture, the hills of Georgia, and well over a hundred thousand miles of hitchhiking. He lives in Atlanta now where he is married to Dawn and works in a warehouse full of metaphysical books.

He became a poet the moment he wrote his first real poem— a hymn of thanks for the moment he was standing in, someplace along the road— and understood that real poems only spring from the things you really care about.

He is active in the Green movement, serves as co-editor of the From Trident to Life Campaign's newsletter and on the editorial committee of the Up & Out of Poverty Now! magazine Street Heat. Because of these concerns, he is sometimes considered a political poet. He is not; it's just that some things really do matter, and poets ignore them at the risk of becoming irrelevant themselves.

He is the author of Crossing the Expressway, an unpublished book of hitchhiking poems. Four-Wheeler & Two-Legged is drawn from a series of chapbooks he photocopied over the years to give away as thanks to all the folks that gave him rides. He typed and designed it himself. Circumstances permitting, he would be honored to read his work to any kind of audience; contact him through the publisher.

Southeastern FRONT

Extra copies of this book can be obtained from Southeastern FRONT. Send $9.95 per copy plus $1 postage and shipping per order to Southeastern FRONT, 565 17th St. NW, Cleveland, Tennessee 37311. Wholesale inquiries are welcome.

Southeastern FRONT is an artists' and writers' presentation/ representation service. Originally designed to provide nationwide exposure for new artists and writers from isolated geographic locales, Southeastern FRONT is now receiving submissions from all over the U.S., Europe and Japan.

In addition to *Four-Wheeler & Two-Legged*, Southeastern FRONT is in the process of publishing *Southeastern FRONT* Magazine, a gallery in a magazine, featuring the best in new art, fiction and poetry. Also in the works is *Southeastern FRONT's Archives of Fiction and Poetry*, an anthology geared toward the major publishing companies' need for fresh material by talented new artists and writers, which has been carefully edited and selected. Please write for information on the availability of these titles upon publication.

A Note on the Typeface

*A*I Prospera*™ is a digital typeface by Peter Fraterdeus. It is an entirely original design, with only minor references to traditional faces, such as the venetians, and a bit of a Clarendon feel in the wide capitals.

Developed with the assistance of a Design Advancement Grant from the National Endowment for the Arts, Prospera is one of the first original type designs to be produced in its entirety on a personal computer, in this case an Apple Macintosh.

The version in use here (2.0) is the first to make use of the recently available PostScript Type 1 hinting and encryption standards, allowing for somewhat crisper letters at text sizes on a low resolution output device (laser printer).

Prospera is available for use with the Macintosh from: Alphabets, Inc. P.O. Box 5448, Evanston, Illinois 60204 • 708 328 2733